YOUR S1 TO DOING THE IMPOSSIBLE

"How a $1 Million Painting, a Vintage Scooter, an Arizona Ghost Town, and Guacamole Can Help You Do Your Impossible 'Cool Thing' Fast."

Your "<u>Cool thing</u>" is the "crazy or impossible" thing you'd love to accomplish.

Dr. Timothy S. Paulson

Published by:
Paulson Creativity Studio, LLC
P.O. Box 41
Tremonton, Utah, 84337
www.PaulsonArtShow.com

Copyright © 2025, Dr. Timothy S. Paulson

Cover Image (painting and photo) by Dr. Timothy S. Paulson

Published in the United States of America

ISBN: 979-8-34660-262-0

No part so this publication may be reproduced in any way without permission and proper attribution to the author of this book.

While every effort has been made to ensure accuracy, the information in this book is provided for general knowledge only and should not be considered a substitute for professional advice. The author and publisher disclaim any liability for errors or omissions, and readers are encouraged to consult appropriate experts regarding their specific situations.

Table of Contents

Your Simple Guide to Doing the Impossible
(a.k.a "Doing your Cool thing")

Foreword iv

Introduction 1

Chapter 1: "The 'Cool thing' of Quickly Becoming a Great Artist" 16

Chapter 2: "The 'Cool thing' of Creating a $120 Million Business" 28

Chapter 3: "The 'Cool thing' of Buying an Arizona Ghost Town" 38

Chapter 4: "The 'Cool thing' of Transforming a $7 Yard-sale Painting into a $1,000,000 Piece of Art" 48

Chapter 5: "Introducing the '7 Cool T' Principles & a Case Study" 62

Conclusion 100

Foreword

If you want to accomplish something big, something remarkable, something some people think is "crazy or impossible" (I refer to that as "your Cool thing") whether in your business or personal life, and it's something you have a burning desire for, you'll love this book because it'll help you get it fast.

I use the term Cool thing to refer to your "crazy and impossible" goal because it's pithy, attention-grabbing, and expressive. Eyes light up, and imaginations fire when people hear it. Hence, this book is about getting your Cool thing to add more enjoyment, achievement, satisfaction, and excitement to your life. Whether it's to double your business, run a marathon, earn a PhD, establish a world-class art collection, start a business, donate a million dollars to your favorite charity, feed the hungry, house the homeless, hike the Himalayas, serve a humanitarian mission, write a book, distribute copies of the Bible worldwide, overcome a significant personal or business challenge, or anything else that's in your heart to do, applying what I've named the "7 Cool T™" principles that I reveal in this book can help you get it.

By the way, I congratulate you on already accomplishing Cool things in your life. You've likely already done things others thought were "crazy or impossible." I wrote this book to help you get your **next** Cool thing (and more Cool things after that) faster and easier than ever.

My first book, Love & Grow Rich: How to Love Your Way to Life's Riches, is over 300 pages long, and my second book, TotalityX: The Art of Becoming All God Created You to Be, is over 200. I'm pleased this book is much shorter because, as Leonardo da Vinci wrote,

"Simplicity is the ultimate sophistication," and I need all the help I can get in the sophistication department. This book is simple, with just this Foreword, an Introduction, and five short chapters. I'm sure some will scoff because of its brevity and simplicity, but those who read with an open mind will enjoy a rewarding adventure filled with valuable insights. I weave the seven principles into the first four chapters; I then fully reveal them in Chapter 5 to provide a unique perspective for accomplishing the "crazy and impossible" in life. While this book stands independent as a resource to help you achieve Cool things in life, it can augment the many fine personal development books you may have read and will read in the future. I trust you'll find high value in applying the "7 Cool T" principles I've identified, named, and introduce in these pages for the first time.

I thank Buck Paulson, Sy Sperling, Joe Polish, and others I write about in this book. I'm also thankful to the likes of Elon Musk, Steve Jobs, Mother Theresa, Martin Luther King, Jr., Pablo Picasso, Michael Jordan, and other historic figures whose lives inform my understanding of how to achieve Cool things. I appreciate them inspiring me to help people achieve their own Cool things.

Finally, I thank my beloved wife, eternal companion, and best friend, Kay, for her never-ending love, support, and inspiration as I continue to go after life's Cool things with her.

Timothy Paulson
Tremonton, Utah

Introduction

A friend of mine named John Raymonds is a highly successful and innovative businessperson and investor. Among other ventures, he was a partner in Bron Studios, the producers of the billion-dollar grossing JOKER (2019) movie. John made a most impactful comment in a Genius Network group meeting a few years ago that has stuck with me and informs the purpose of this book. He said that when his friend, the famed innovator Peter Diamandis, who founded the XPRIZE, shared his vision to extend the XPRIZE model to the domain of education, John responded, **"That sounds impossible. How can I help?"**

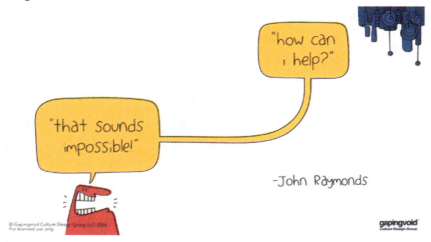

Don't you just love John's response? When I heard it, it went straight to my heart and inspired me. It's both incredulous and eager, and a variation nicely summarizes the purpose of this book: **"Your Cool thing sounds impossible. I can help."**

This book is written to enhance the quality of your business and life, help you have more fun, increase your happiness, facilitate greater accomplishment, and even help clarify your life's purpose by pursuing and achieving your next <u>Cool thing</u>.

For fun, let's begin by considering what "cool" even means. It's not easy to define, but you kind of know it when you see it, right? For me, The Beatles and the Bible are cool; creating a new painting in my art studio is cool; art by Jackson Pollock and Vincent van Gogh is cool; philanthropy is cool; serving and helping others become their best selves through personal and spiritual development is cool; interfaith unity is cool; marriage with my eternal companion Kay and having children and grandchildren is very cool; and being loved by and having faith in Jesus Christ is totally cool! Really, "cool" means something different to each of us.

I like the following AI generated definition of "cool":

> "Coolness, or being cool, is an aesthetic of attitude, behavior, comportment, appearance, and style that is generally admired. Because of the varied and changing interpretation of what is considered cool, as well as its subjective nature, the word has no single meaning."

In preparation for a big Halloween party during my senior year in high school, I joked with my friends, "I'm going to the party as a 'cool dude' so I can just go as myself." I had a shirt printed with "Too Cool Paulson" on the back that I wore to the party. I don't know how many people were humored by it, but it was an attempt, even in jest, to be a bit more "cool."

"What's your Cool thing?"

Again, your Cool thing (I sometimes abbreviate it as "Cool T") is the term I use for that thing in your heart that is fascinating, unique, crazy, and seemingly impossible, that you have a burning desire to accomplish in your business or in your personal life. It could even include something you might call your "passion project."

I've spent over 40 years in the business world and enjoy helping business leaders, entrepreneurs, and others bring their Cool things to fruition. For example, in Chapter 2, I'll tell you about a famous entrepreneur I helped get his Cool thing, which was creating a $100+ million company (and doing inspiring philanthropic work as well).

In addition to possibilities I've already mentioned, your business or personal "Cool thing" could be anything, perhaps even one of the following:

- Increase your business by $1 million, $10 million, $100 million, or more
- Write a screenplay that's made into a movie
- Lose "a ton" of weight
- Start a successful podcast or television show
- Ride across the country on a scooter
- Travel to space
- Take your dream vacation
- Set a world record in something

- Start some philanthropic activity
- Do something to increase peace, love, and unity in the world

The sky's the limit! This list is just the very "tip of the iceberg" of possible <u>Cool things</u> you could choose to pursue.

In my business I'm an author, speaker, coach, business consultant, and artist who sells my paintings. In fact, one of my next <u>Cool things</u> is to sell what once was a dusty and boring $7 yard-sale painting – one I bought and transformed into the colorful and explosive abstract painting you see on the cover of this book – for $1 million (I'll tell you all about it in Chapter 4). When the million-dollar painting sells, it'll be a catalyst for another <u>Cool thing</u> I'm going after, which is to develop a new Art Movement (like famous Art Movements that have been informed by the work of Picasso, Monet, Pollock, and others), with the objective to create significant social impact.

One of the principles I advance in this book is, "If you want to do something great, stop waiting for permission." I have zero interest in waiting for permission to do my <u>Cool things</u>. Perhaps it's time for you to stop waiting for permission to move forward with yours, too.

"My 1964 vintage scooter helps illustrate the <u>Cool thing</u> philosophy"

Though it's too insignificant a thing to fit my working definition of a <u>Cool thing</u>, my vintage scooter that appears on the cover of this book with my $1 million painting is still cool. The cover reads, "How a $1 Million Painting, a Vintage Scooter, an Arizona Ghost Town, and Guacamole Can Help You Do Your Impossible 'Cool Thing' Fast." Ironically, the story of how I bought the scooter helps to frame, in a fun way, the "7 Cool T" principles that'll help you get your next Cool thing.

"My Scooters"

I accidently stumbled onto a "for sale" ad for a modern scooter some time ago. I'd never considered buying a scooter before, but my wife and I were just about to move to a small town in Utah, and I envisioned riding the scooter around town after moving. I bought it, and what I envisioned has come to full fruition – I love riding a scooter to the gym, stores, the post office, and around the neighborhood to meet and greet people and explore the area.

My modern scooter

A short time after moving, I, for fun, joined a scooter group on Facebook and quickly became friends with some of the members online. One of the group's administrators reached out and invited me to come to an "Italian Fest" in Salt Lake City a few days later to see a display of vintage scooters that some in the group were involved in.

Accepting the invitation, I went to the festival, met some very cool people, and admired their beautiful vintage scooters.

Me with some of the vintage scooters on display in SLC

Seeing the vintage scooters stimulated my interest in owning one, so I enquired and learned that one of the group's leaders named Benny had a 1964 model for sale. He showed me photos of the beautiful red scooter, and I wanted it. Unfortunately, Benny said a guy from Idaho was already in the process of buying it, and he had agreed to hold it for him as long as he sent a deposit to secure it. But Benny hadn't received any money yet, so there was hope I could buy it.

I anxiously texted Benny the next morning to check the status of the sale. He responded that he still hadn't received money from the guy in Idaho but was going to reach out to give him one last chance.

A few hours later, Benny texted me that he hadn't heard back from the guy, and if I wanted it, I could buy it. I didn't hesitate and immediately sent the money for the scooter. (By the way, in the '50s and '60s, scooters made and distributed in Italy by the Piaggio Company were called "Vespa," and those distributed in the United States through the

Sears & Roebuck company were called "Allstate." My 1964 scooter has a cool Allstate badge, and I refer to it as both an Allstate and a Vespa.)

Benny later showed me his text exchange with the potential buyer in Idaho. The guy's name is Chris, and I saw that he wrote to Benny, "It's getting late, how about we finish this up tomorrow?" However, his failure to follow up the next day and the day after is what caused Chris to miss out. I was decisive; I took action; I knew what I wanted and didn't wait.

When he delivered the scooter to my home, I asked Benny if he ever heard back from Chris. Benny said yes and that Chris was in tears when he heard that the scooter had been sold to someone else. I felt sorry for Chris, but it's a lesson to be decisive. In fact, #7 of the "7 Cool T" principles I'll fully introduce in Chapter 5 is "Be Decisive."

Me on my vintage scooter after my first ride

The humorous rest of the story is that I had to explain to my wife Kay that I bought a second scooter. When I did, she calmly responded, "Do you remember what I said when you went to the Italian Fest? 'Don't buy another scooter'."

Well, #6 of the "7 Cool T" principles advanced in this book is "Don't Wait for Permission" (much more on that later).

"This scooter is cool"

I bought the beautiful vintage scooter because it's cool and because, as a marketer and an artist who sells my paintings, I could see value in using it to help differentiate and promote my work. I also knew that I could write about it (as I have in this book), paint pictures inspired by it (which I have), coach and speak in seminars about it to help illustrate business success principles (as I did in Nashville, as you can see in the following photo).

Me speaking of my vintage scooter at a seminar in Nashville, TN

As expected, rolling the scooter into my art studio created a different atmosphere and "framed" my art in photographs, including my most recent "Statute of Liberty" painting, which you can see in the photos that follow.

My "Statue of Liberty" painting (36"x36")

You can see these photos, along with pictures of several more paintings, in my online gallery at www.PaulsonArtShow.com.

The vintage scooter is fun to ride around town, to meet people on, and to start all kinds of conversations with. It attracts attention wherever I go and helps to set me apart as "different" in my business as an artist, author, coach, business consultant, and speaker (a quote I'll introduce to you later is "It's better to be different than it is to be better"). In fact, "Be Different" is #3 of the "7 Cool T" principles I'll be sharing with you.

I've used the scooter to promote other works of art as well, including my "Beatles Sculpture" and "Johnny Cash: Ring of Fire," as you can see in the following photos.

My "Ring of Fire" painting of Johnny Cash at Folsom Prison, 1966 (36"x36")

My "Beatles Sculpture" (with John, Paul, George & Ringo, painted on a tree stump) sitting on the back of the scooter

Though buying a vintage scooter is a small thing compared to what you may have in mind, the following ideas and principles begin to emerge through the story:

- Your <u>Cool thing</u> can be whatever you want it to be.

- Know what makes you <u>happy</u>. Know what makes your heart sing. What do you want to spend time with? (I sometimes leave my art studio during the day for a quick ride on the vintage scooter because it's so fun and makes me feel like a kid.)

- Being <u>different</u> is a fundamental principle to achieving <u>Cool things</u> (#3 of the "<u>7 Cool T</u>").

- <u>Don't wait for permission</u> to go after your <u>Cool things</u> (#6 of the "7 Cool T").

- Being <u>decisive</u> is also another critical success principle (#7 of the "<u>7 Cool T</u>").

The story of my getting the scooter applies to you getting your <u>Cool thing</u> – and mine too (which I'll tell you about in Chapter 4).

"In this short book..."

In the first four chapters of this book, I share stories of some remarkable individuals who will inspire you to accomplish your next <u>Cool thing.</u> Then, in Chapter 5, I fully reveal the seven principles that will help you to do so.

Four people I'll tell you about, along with their <u>Cool things</u>, are:

1. **A former minor-league baseball player with no apparent artistic talent who achieved his next <u>Cool thing</u> by becoming a Master Artist.** You may be familiar with the artist because he's had his own TV show on PBS since 1988. You know – you scroll through the channels on the television, and you stop for a few minutes to admire an artist on the screen who's painting. Well, that's my dad. (No, I'm not

referring to the artist on TV with the "big hair" – that's Bob Ross. The artist I write of in Chapter 1 is Buck Paulson, and his show is titled "Painting with Paulson.")

2. **A streetfighter from the Bronx, NY, who some thought was the least likely person to become the colossal business success he became.** His famous advertising tagline, "I'm not only the Hair Club president, but I'm also a client," made him a household name in the '80s and '90s. In Chapter 2, I'll tell you about how my friend, Sy Sperling, got his <u>Cool thing</u> of creating a business empire.

3. **A formerly drug-addicted & dead-broke Carpet Cleaner who is now a multi-millionaire and one of the best-connected entrepreneurs in the U.S.** He's my friend Joe Polish. In Chapter 3, I'll tell you about Joe's remarkable business and about the <u>Cool thing</u> he did of buying a 40-acre ghost town in Arizona called Cleator, and what it means to you.

4. **My own <u>Cool things</u> of transforming a $7 yard-sale painting into a $1 million painting** – and working to develop "**the New Art Movement of the 21st Century**" to make social impact, which I share in Chapter 4.

Most importantly, in Chapter 5, I'll show you how the "<u>7 Cool T</u>" principles revealed in the successes of Buck Paulson, Sy Sperling, Joe Polish, and myself apply to <u>you</u> achieving your <u>Cool thing</u> in your business or personal life because that's what this book is all about. In the same chapter, I'll also tell you the "Guacamole Story" in a Case Study about a Mexican Restaurant that applies to you.

Now, before you go on, please take a few minutes to answer the following question:

"What's your <u>Cool thing</u>?"

<u>To stimulate your thinking on what your next "Cool thing" is, consider the following questions:</u>

What would you like to **create**? What would you like to **buy**? What would you like to **give**? Where where would you like to **travel**? What would you like to **invent**? What would you like to **do**? What would you like to **collect**? How would you like to **serve** your community? What would you like to **improve**? Where would you like to **worship**? What **spiritual growth** would you like to get? Where would you like to **live**? Whose **lives** do you want to help improve, and how? What would you like to **read**? What would you like to **see**? What would you like to **advance** or **promote**? What or who would you like to **lead**? What **social impact** would you like to make?

You may not get your answer exactly right just yet, but please play along in the following helpful exercise because it'll get your creative juices flowing. Go ahead and write below ideas that come to mind, then, choose one from that list as your next <u>Cool thing</u>.

Brainstorm:

Write some potential <u>Cool things</u> you'd like to get next.

_____
_____
_____
_____
_____
_____
_____
_____

Now choose your next <u>Cool thing</u> from the list.

_____
_____
_____
_____
_____

Chapter 1: "The Cool thing of Quickly Becoming a Great Artist"

> "Let's see if we can make a great artist out of you in a year." - Claude Buck

My dad is a former pro baseball player who "beat the odds" to become a full-time professional artist with his own show on PBS television starting in 1988. His story is remarkable because he had never painted before deciding to become an artist at the age of 27.

First, some background. He's Don Paulson, known professionally as the artist Buck Paulson, who grew up on a farm in a small Minnesota town called Pelican Rapids. He is one of five children in his family, with his world as a youth completely revolving around playing sports as he lettered in baseball, basketball, and football in high school. Dad was most accomplished as a baseball pitcher and wanted to play pro baseball after his high school graduation. But after asking Dad to hold up his hands so he could see them, his high school counselor said his hands were too small to play professional baseball and discouraged him from pursuing such an impossible goal. But Dad knew what he wanted (playing pro ball was his first Cool thing). After graduating at the age of 17, his burning desire took him to a tryout with a minor league baseball team called the Fargo-Morehead Twins of the Class-C Northern League.

The Twins were in the Cleveland Indians organization and had just hired a new manager, Danny Litwhiler, who had played 11 years in the Major Leagues including in two World Series. Litwhiler's accolades include his glove being on display in the Baseball Hall of Fame in Cooperstown, NY, as the first player ever to play an entire season in the Major Leagues without committing an error; he is also acknowledged in the Hall of Fame for being the inventor of the Speed Gun's use in baseball; he managed the Florida State and Michigan State University baseball teams and in 1980 was inducted into the College Baseball Hall of Fame as a manager.

Dad in 1952 as a professional baseball player with the Fargo-Morehead Twins

At the tryout in 1952, Litwhiler watched as Dad threw pitches and was impressed enough to give him a contract, making Dad the youngest player on the team.

Something memorable from that team is that Dad roomed briefly with teammate Roger Maris, the same guy who later played for the New York Yankees and broke Babe Ruth's Major League single-season home-run record with 61. Another is that Dad's team played against the Eau Claire Bears, a team that featured a young power-hitting shortstop named Hank Aaron, who went on to break Babe Ruth's career Major League home-run record with 755.

Dad later played for the "Fort Walton Beach Jets" and the "Baton Rouge Red Sticks" baseball clubs. He left baseball to serve in the U.S. Army, and after his service, met my mom at Brigham Young University, married, and graduated with a degree in Physical Education. My parents moved to Vauxhall, Alberta, Canada, where Dad taught at Vauxhall High School, coached the high school basketball and baseball teams, and played pro baseball with the Vauxhall Jets. A couple of years later, he got a job as a Recreation Department Supervisor in beautiful Santa Barbara, California. Mom was from there, and Dad had previously played a season for the Santa Barbara Foresters, a semi-pro team on which he was given the "Best Pitcher" award.

A news clipping including Dad (pictured on the right) while playing with the Santa Barbara Foresters

I provide that background to show that Dad pivoting to become a full-time artist would have seemed highly unlikely.

"An Artist? Really?"

Dad got a "D" grade in the only art class he ever took in school. He was an athlete through and through, with little interest in anything else. (It may have surprised some people when my mom, a beautiful and vivacious Theatre Arts major in college, married such a jock.)

Shortly after moving to Santa Barbara in 1962 to start his new job, Dad stopped one day to admire the work of an artist who was painting along the sidewalk. Dad was drawn to the work and later visited the artist in his studio to see more of his paintings. Something began to stir within Dad, and he came home one day and said to Mom, "I want to be an artist."

This must have shocked Mom because it was so foreign to anything he had ever been interested in. "What does art have to do with sports?" she might have wondered.

Mom, an eternal optimist, was completely supportive and told Dad she'd buy him an art kit for his birthday. But Dad didn't want to wait, so he went to a local art store and bought his first art supplies. Excitedly, he sat at the kitchen table and painted a tree on a paper towel, shown below.

Dad's first painting, 1962

Dad refers to the tree painting as his "First Attempt." Years later he asked my older sister, Dondi, how old she though he was when he painted the picture of the tree. Dondi replied, "Three?" He was 27 years old.

Dad planned to take adult education classes to learn how to paint, but in a fortuitous visit to the gallery of an artist named Kitty West, she told him, "You aren't going to learn anything in those adult education classes. If you want to learn to paint, go to the master. His name is Claude Buck." Kitty said she didn't know if Buck was accepting any new students, but she gave him Claude's contact information and suggested he inquire.

Not wasting any time, Dad drove right over to Claude Buck's home at 1114 N. Milpas Street and knocked on the door. Leslie Buck answered and directed my inquiring dad to the backyard where her husband was painting.

Claude Buck's former home at
1114 N. Milpas St. in Santa Barbara

"Who was Claude Buck?"

Claude Buck was a child prodigy in art. He was born in 1890 and, at the age of eleven, was the youngest person ever to be given a copyist license at the Metropolitan Museum of Art and was also the youngest ever to attend the National Academy of Design. Claude was later recognized by the Arts Council of New York as one of the one-hundred best living American painters. He had been an artist his entire life, having studied with well-known instructors at prestigious art schools. Originally from New York and having lived for many years in Chicago, where he taught at the Chicago Academy of Fine Art and the Art Institute, Claude moved to Santa Barbara three years before the fateful meeting with my dad.

Upon meeting Claude, Dad expressed that he had never painted before but wanted to be an artist. Claude didn't ask for a resume; he didn't ask to see samples of his work; he didn't ask for references; he didn't ask where he went to school; he didn't ask about his family. After speaking with Dad, Claude said something totally unexpected:

"Let's see if we can make a great artist out of you in a year."

These 15 words changed Dad's life forever. Claude was no neophyte, nor was he subject to hyperbole. He was a 72-year-old master artist and teacher who knew what it took to become a great artist. Claude knew it started with the burning desire he saw in Dad and that it would come to fruition with the quality instruction and support he would provide.

Dad's next Cool thing was to quickly go from being a complete novice to becoming a great artist.

Claude Buck and Dad

After completing his first painting with Claude's guidance, Dad wanted to show respect for and honor Claude, so he asked him if he could sign his paintings "Buck Paulson" and use that as his artist name. Claude was pleased and graciously consented. With Claude's help, Dad did indeed become a great artist, later resigning his position at the Recreation Department to become a full-time professional artist when I was still a young boy.

"The Master had his young protégé's back"

Claude Buck believed in Dad and was his advocate. One of my favorite stories is from the mid 1960s when Dad submitted a painting to be considered for inclusion in the Santa Barbara Art Association show. The painting he submitted was rejected by the jury, an action that annoyed Claude because he knew Dad's painting was more than worthy to be included in the show. Claude invited Dad to go with him as he marched down to the office of the mayor of Santa Barbara with Dad's painting in tow. Claude showed the painting to the mayor, W. Don MacGillivray, and asked him if he thought anything was wrong with it. The mayor responded, "Absolutely not," adding that the painting was "Magnificent!" Claude informed the mayor that the jury for the Santa Barbara Art Association show rejected the painting. Incredulous, the mayor called a meeting to discuss the painting and the jury's decision. The decision was reversed, and the painting was accepted into the art show. Dad later became highly respected by members of the Art Association, but they held a bit of a grudge against Claude because of this interaction. Claude didn't care because his interest was always in doing the right thing, including advocating for Dad on his path to becoming a great full-time artist.

"It's better to be different, than it is to be better"

Author and Hall of Fame speaker Sally Hogshead has said, "It's better to be different, than it is to be better." She adds, "Being better is good, but being different is better." Dad, too, has become a master artist and teacher who has differentiated himself in various ways. Dad is different by not just dabbling in art as most artists in the world do – he showed a burning desire and determination by becoming a full-time artist when he had a wife and five young kids to provide for. Additionally, though Claude Buck rarely painted a seascape and didn't spend much time teaching Dad how to do it, Dad has become known as "Master of the High Seas" for his gorgeous seascapes; he has merged his love for sports and art at times by painting some fantasy pieces with baseball players subtly painted in the clouds of seascapes; he has been teaching on TV since 1988; he is outgoing and generous with his students; he forever honors his teacher, Claude Buck; he always puts God first in his art and his life.

You've likely seen Buck Paulson on television. He's not as well-known as the artist Bob Ross, but Dad actually has the record for the most years of producing new art shows for PBS television.

Buck Paulson in his studio with a seascape and his "First Attempt" painting below it (photo courtesy of Buck Paulson)

Today, at the age of 90, Dad continues to paint six days a week while producing masterful paintings, and his art business continues as he sells his art and teaches multiple weekly online art classes through the Alexander Art Company.

You can see his work at www.BuckPaulson.com.

Dad has achieved the Cool things of becoming a professional baseball player and a great artist. In addition, his most significant Cool thing is his remarkable 66-year marriage to Mom, his love for and complete devotion to God, and an admiring posterity who absolutely loves and honors him.

Now, because I want all I'm sharing to apply to you, go ahead and complete the following statement as if directed to you:

> "Let's see if we can make a great _____ out of you in a year."

How would you fill in the blank in the above statement? Try inserting your Cool thing and see what it looks like. As I've already mentioned, for me (as you'll read all about in Chapter 4), it is:

"Let's see if we can sell my $1 million painting in a year."

"Let's see if we can develop a new Art Movement in a year."

Dad and me recently together in his Santa Barbara, CA studio

Though some doubted him, Dad went forward with the instruction and encouragement of the masters who believed in him in both baseball and in art. Dad didn't get his Cool things by himself. He wouldn't have become a professional baseball player without the help of Danny Litwhiler (they remained dear friends until Litwhiler's passing in 2011 at the age of 95). And he never would have become a great artist without the help of Claude Buck. You can't get most Cool things by yourself, either, and I wrote this book to share the "7 Cool T" principles to help.

In Chapter 5, I'll tell you more about Dad's path to becoming a great artist by applying the seven principles in his life and how you can apply them in your life, too.

How does Buck Paulson's
<u>Cool things</u> inspire you to get yours?

Chapter 2: "The <u>Cool thing</u> of Creating a $120 Million Business"

"I'm Not Only the Hair Club President,
But I'm Also a Client." – Sy Sperling

Sy Sperling was the famous founder and president of <u>Hair Club for Men</u>®. I served as Vice President of Sales for the company during years of momentous growth, where I had a front-row seat to Sy's <u>Cool thing</u> coming to fruition (I'll tell you all about it) – it was remarkable to be a part of.

Sy Sperling and me in my home, 1995

As founder and president of <u>Hair Club for Men</u>, Sy Sperling was a household name back in the '80s and '90s, having become famous through his advertising tagline on his seemingly ubiquitous television commercials. In his commercials, he held up his bald "before" photo and said in his New York accent, **"I'm not only the Hair Club president, but I'm also a client."**

Sy grew up in a lower-class family in the Bronx, NY. He told me many stories of how when young, he didn't have much interest in anything other than street-fighting, playing pranks and sports, the New York Yankees, and girls. He was often in trouble at school for the pranks he pulled on teachers and students alike, for being disruptive, and for being a goof-off. After graduating high school, Sy served in the U.S. Army and later became a swimming pool salesman. His older brother, Jay, introduced him to the hair replacement industry which Sy entered in the late '60s, and in 1976, Sy astutely named his company Hair Club for Men.

In 1986, I flew from California to meet with Sy in his offices in New York City, where he interviewed me for the job of helping to open and run his new Hair Club office in Chicago. We "clicked" right away, and he told me within just seven minutes of meeting, "I've already made my decision. I want to hire you for Chicago." During my interview, Sy told me of his background, including his street fighting days in the Bronx and the big things he intended to accomplish in business. (By the way, Sy liked it when I told him he reminded me of Sylvester Stallone.) He said, "Some people think I'm crazy, but we're gonna' do $100 mil a year someday. We're doing about ten mil now, with nine offices. But I want to have 20, 30, 40, then 50 and more offices." I said, "That's cool." He paused, smiled, then responded, "It's very cool!" I said, "That's pretty good for a street fighter from the Bronx."

Later, a friend of Sy's dropped in and told us *Saturday Night Live* had done a skit on Sy and Hair Club on its last show. I confess that it made me nervous about working for the company because, apparently, it was being mocked and made fun of on national TV. But Sy was ecstatic. "Are you kidding me? That's fantastic," he said. "Do you know how much it would cost to run a commercial on *Saturday Night Live*? That's gonna' be great for business!" Sy proved correct about that because he understood the power of publicity. He later became a frequent guest on shows like *Saturday Night Live*, *The Tonight Show*, and many other well-known programs.

After my interview, Sy and I walked the streets in Manhattan, with one person after another recognizing him and yelling out, "Hey, it's Sy Sperling," and "Hey, you're the Hair Club for Men president," and "Hey, you're not only the president, but you're also a client." Sy welcomed the recognition, knowing it was good for business. Sy declared his hair loss and hair replacement without reservation on national TV, bringing dignity and acceptance to the concept of men improving their appearance.

Sy did hire me for the Chicago office. I later opened and operated three more Hair Club offices in Maryland and Virginia. I was eventually promoted to Vice President of Sales, and during the time I worked with Sy, the company expanded to 69 offices and grew to around $120 million a year in sales, an increase of over $100 million a year from when I started working with him. Sy well exceeded the Cool thing he had told me about when I first met him; Hair Club for Men offices dotted the country with sales exceeding $100 million a year as he had predicted. Many people doubted Sy could ever pull off such a

30

thing, but he certainly got his Cool thing and, in the year 2000, sold the company for tens of millions of dollars.

In Sy's words, that's very cool!

Sy Sperling and me in the
Chicago Hair Club office, 1987

"Sy's famous tag line"

In the late '70s and early '80s, Sy's Hair Club for Men advertising included celebrities who were Hair Club clients who gave endorsements for the product. For example, Ron Blomberg and Joe Pepitone, who had played for the New York Yankees, and Billy Smith and Chico Resch, who played for the New York Islanders hockey team, appeared as clients in print ads. Sy also used some of his "regular clients" in before and after advertisements. The ads were effective in generating business, but everything changed dramatically for the better when Sy decided to make a TV commercial. A man named Berton Miller produced the commercial and, while filming, suggested that, as a backup to the main commercial they were filming, Sy personally appear in a secondary commercial and say at the end, "I'm not only the Hair Club president, but I'm also a client" while unexpectedly holding up his bald "before" picture. Sy told me he didn't care for the idea at first, but decided to take a chance and went ahead and recorded the alternate commercial. As it turned out, the first commercial bombed, while the commercial with the "I'm also a client" tagline was an immediate hit! The phone rang off the hook in response to the commercial, business went through the roof, and an iconic advertising tagline was born.

"Sy was fueled by the difficulty of the task"

Sy was clear on what he wanted – the "crazy" business growth that seemed impossible to others but that he envisioned and believed would come to fruition. He could have kept his business small with a few offices in the New York City area, which would have provided him a good living. It surely would have been easier to stay small because growing a national company with scores of offices is exceedingly complex. However, as I participated in the company's growth and closely observed Sy, I realized it was the difficulty of the task itself that often fueled his energy and passion.

Sy had to overcome plenty of obstacles along the way. One of the biggest was that the CEO he hired in the late '80s turned out to be largely incompetent. The CEO made so many poor decisions and created so much dysfunction in the company that it led to crippling debt that nearly put Hair Club out of business. Sy fired the CEO and for a time brought in a "turnaround specialist" named Eitan to help navigate the debt and "right the ship." But Sy and Eitan rarely saw eye to eye and frequently butted heads. In fact, one day I was in a room with both Sy and Eitan in Hair Club's corporate offices when the discussion became heated, and Sy, who was standing, got nose to nose with Eitan, who was sitting, screaming in his face. I saw "the street fighter from the Bronx" come out in Sy and expected fists to fly. But Sy was in total control and later told me he deliberately created a scene to make a point, successfully leading to his desired result. Through Sy's leadership, marketing savvy, and pure determination, the company recovered and succeeded more than ever.

"It's better to be different, than it is to be better"

A big reason for Sy's success is that he did things so differently from the rest of the hair industry. He had a clear vision and instinctively knew he couldn't achieve the "impossible" by being the same as everyone else. While most hair replacement companies had names such as "John's Hair Replacement," Sy called his company <u>Hair Club for Men</u>, a brilliant move because the name represented a friendly place where men could feel good about getting their hair taken care of. And where most hair replacement businesses were located in storefronts or in barber shops, Sy put his <u>Hair Club for Men</u> offices into beautiful office buildings with well-trained and well-compensated professional employees. Starting out, Sy's product wasn't any better than what other companies offered. But over time, his product became better, and he uniquely trademarked it as <u>The Strand-by-Strand System</u>®. Sy hired highly talented stylists and consultants and paid them well to ensure the clients were well taken care of. His vision of what <u>Hair Club for Men</u> could become could only be accomplished with the right people helping him. Also, instead of avoiding the camera and publicity,

Sy was front and center in advocating his company on every television commercial and on countless television and radio interviews. Finally, it's inspiring that instead of just talking about doing good in the community, Sy took action and started a charity called Hair Club for Kids®, through which the company, then and now, provides its hair process to kids aged 6-17 who have lost their hair through medical treatment and for other reasons – all free of charge.

I worked with Sy until 1995, at which time I resigned to start my own business as a motivational speaker, coach, and business consultant. A decade later, Sy and I got together in Florida to record conversations centered around the topic of How to Succeed in Business Beyond Your Wildest Dreams. We did the recordings more as an excuse to get together and reminisce than anything. It was fun and inspiring to hear more of Sy's stories of how he raised himself from rags to riches in achieving the "impossible."

Sy and me recording our "How to Succeed in Business Beyond Your Wildest Dreams" conversations in Florida in 2005

Sy was one of the most wonderful and hilarious persons I've ever known, and he and I remained great friends until his passing in 2020.

Sy and me in Vancouver in 2019

I love Sy and will always appreciate our friendship and how he inspired me through his goodness and huge accomplishments. He was a faithful Jewish man, and he and his wife, Susan, gave generously to the community, including funding a Hebrew school in Ft. Lauderdale, while always being so kind and respectful of me and my Christian beliefs. I'm forever grateful he showed me how to achieve Cool things.

In Chapter 5, I'll tell you more about Sy's path to creating his business empire by applying each of the "7 Cool T" principles – and how you can apply them, too.

How does Sy Sperling's <u>Cool thing</u> inspire yours?

_____
_____
_____
_____
_____
_____
_____
_____
_____
_____
_____
_____
_____
_____
_____
_____
_____

Chapter 3: "The <u>Cool thing</u> of Buying an Arizona Ghost Town"

"Want to buy a town?" -Jason Campbell

It's not every day you have a friend who buys a ghost town. It was while having lunch with Joe Polish in Salt Lake City in November of 2021, that he dropped the news that he was buying a town called Cleator, AZ. He showed me photos of the town, which immediately lit my imagination. Talk about a <u>Cool thing</u> – buying a 40-acre ghost town in Arizona qualifies.

An aerial shot of Joe Polish and me walking with his partners in the ghost town of Cleator, AZ (photo courtesy of Joe Polish)

Cleator is in Yavapai County, AZ, has twenty simple structures, and according to a hand-written sign in Cleator, has "eight residents, five dogs and two grumpy cats." The town is located on a rough dirt road leading to Crown King and is the home of the "Cleator Bar and Yacht Club" (you read that right – Cleator has a yacht club in the middle of the desert [more on that later]).

Shortly after Joe and his three business partners (Jason Campbell, Mike Leoni, and Ben Hudye) closed on the purchase of the town in January 2022, I eagerly drove from my home in Utah for a personal visit to Cleator.

Me at the old Cleator schoolhouse before renovations

I was awe-struck as I drove my truck into town – it was as if I'd gone back in time. It was fun to walk the town, meet some long-time residents, enter original frontier buildings, and enjoy the town's ambiance. The place is just plain cool.

"Who is this Joe Polish guy?"

I met Joe Polish in 1997 at a large business seminar in Phoenix. As soon as he walked into the room, Joe's presence was felt through his energy, effervescent personality, humor, his self-proclaimed moniker of "an obnoxious marketing genius," and his ponytail. Though Joe no longer sports a ponytail (or any hair for that matter), and years ago did away with the "obnoxious genius" moniker, the positive impact he makes wherever he goes has grown exponentially.

Joe has brought to fruition many Cool things in his career. For example, he founded and leads Genius Network® and 100K Group®, two of the highest-level connection, discussion, and marketing networks for entrepreneurs on the planet (masterminding also occurs in the groups, but there's vastly more to them than that). The website is www.GeniusNetwork.com. Joe is remarkably big-hearted and, after almost dying from drug addiction as a teenager, he years later founded a nonprofit called Genius Recovery® to help addicts and to change the global conversation about addiction. Joe is an example of one who believes business profit is good, but profit used for good is better. He also curates the annual Genius Network Event with famous guests like RFK Jr., Jordan Peterson, Tony Robbins, and several hundred high-level entrepreneurs in attendance each year. Joe is known as one of the best connectors in the business world and has the unique ability to put the right people together to create "entrepreneurial magic." One example was when, back in 2004, Joe invited me to co-create with him an audio program titled Piranha Marketing: The 7 Success Multiplying Factors to Dominate any Market You Enter, published by Nightingale-Conant. We are fortunate that it turned out to be the best-selling marketing program Nightingale-Conant ever created in its long history.

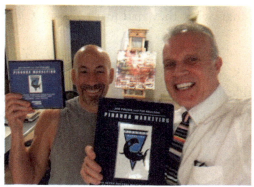

Joe Polish and me in a recent photo with the
#1 best-selling marketing program we co-created

Over a 20-year period, I had the privilege of helping Joe bring some of his "crazy and impossible" ideas – his <u>Cool things</u> – to fruition in his business. And now, Joe buying a ghost town is one of the coolest.

"Buying the ghost town"

Joe took a year sabbatical from his business in 2021 (the sabbatical is yet another <u>Cool thing</u> he did), during which he received a text one morning from his good friend, Jason Campbell.

Jason's text kind of jokingly said, "Want to buy a town?"

The text included a link to information about Cleator, AZ, being for sale.

Joe texted back, "Maybe."

It wasn't long before things got serious and Joe and his partners purchased Cleator. Interestingly, shortly after the sale, Joe and his partners were contacted by someone who had been considering buying Cleator but procrastinated and missed out. The person offered

$250,000 more than what they had just paid for Cleator, which they rejected.

Now, is buying a ghost town "crazy or impossible?" It's probably more "improbable" than "impossible" – but yes, it is kind of "crazy." The purchase helps to illustrate the "7 Cool T" principles, including Joe and his partners being decisive in buying the town, which again illustrates a principle for getting your Cool thing: "Be Decisive."

Since purchasing Cleator, the new owners have beautifully and meticulously remodeled the old schoolhouse, dug the first water well the town's ever had, created an "art fence" with 100+ year old mining equipment, put Cleator into "Virtual Reality," created a Cleator NFT (Non-fungible token), created The Cleator Times, rented out the property for events, and trademarked the name "Cleator Ghost Town™." (You may even see copies of the book you're reading right now for sale in the Cleator General Store.)

"Coming off sabbatical"

Joe's Genius Network and 100K Group members missed him during his year-long sabbatical, and at his February 2022 Genius Network Annual Event, there was a celebration for his return from his time away. I helped emcee the beginning of the event, and there was a palpable buzz in the audience as I stood on stage to welcome the crowd and to start the event. When Joe stepped on stage to a huge welcome and thunderous applause from the 400+ attendees, he told the story about buying Cleator, which astonished the audience. He then made it all applicable to the audience by asking, "What's *your* Cleator?" meaning, "Identify a big idea or opportunity worth exploring for you." Joe has done a masterful job coining and utilizing the question in Genius Network ever since.

A photo I took from backstage of Joe (on the right) with one of his partners, Jason Campbell (on the left). They stood on the stage as Cleator's symbolic "Mayor" (Joe), and "Sheriff" (Jason)

Later, I authored a report titled "What's Your Cleator? A Story of Big Ideas," which Joe distributes at www.WhatsYourCleator.com. As I considered what more I can do to inspire people to do big things, the idea of this book emerged. As I've worked on it and my thoughts and understanding have expanded, I've identified and named the "7 Cool T" principles I share in Chapter 5. I appreciate Joe and his ghost town helping to inspire the creation of this book so I can help you achieve your "craziest and most impossible" goals – your Cool thing – more decisively.

Joe Polish and me laughing together on stage at his February 2022 <u>Genius Network Annual Event</u>

"It's better to be different, than it is to be better."

I repeat Sally Hogshead's statements, "It's better to be different than it is to be better," and "It's good to be better, but it's better to be different." Joe introduced me to Sally through <u>Genius Network</u>, and I love her statements because they provide valuable insight, and Joe personifies them. For example, when he started out teaching Carpet Cleaners how to market more successfully, Joe had competition in the space. Others teaching in the industry were more traditional and came across as professional and conservative. Joe was both <u>better and different.</u> He came along with his superior marketing expertise, creativity, a brash attitude, and a more casual approach including having a ponytail, and took the industry by storm. Joe's marketing said that he was "An obnoxious marketing genius who can help you double your Carpet Cleaning business in 90 days." He was highly successful in helping thousands of Carpet Cleaners take their businesses to the next level, and they loved him for it.

Additionally, Joe was the first and only person in the Cleaning industry who held annual "Marketing Boot Camps" with up to 600 attendees and guest speakers that included the likes of Sir Richard Branson (who appeared via satellite), singer Paula Abdul, professional athletes, and famous authors like Robert Kiyosaki ("Rich Dad, Poor Dad"), Mark Victor Hansen ("Chicken Soup for the Soul"), David Bach ("The Automatic Millionaire"), Bill Phillips ("Body for Life"), Dan Kennedy ("No BS Marketing") and many others. Joe boldly stepped up to become the master coach and marketer the industry looked to. I witnessed the self-image of Carpet Cleaners and their feelings about the industry improve dramatically when Joe brought celebrities and famous authors to his events. Joe was also different when he started a high-level discussion and mastermind group for Carpet Cleaners, a program I helped him develop and run called Platinum Plus, which cost members $10,000-$15,000 a year to belong to. I can see that for Joe, being better has always been good, but being different makes him even better. And now, Joe has differentiated himself further by buying a ghost town.

"You can't do it alone"

Joe would be the first person to tell you he didn't get his Cool things alone, including purchasing Cleator. Claude Buck helped Buck Paulson, and Sy Sperling, Joe Polish, and I have had plenty of help in our journeys. None of us would have achieved what we have on our own. We began by "going to the masters" for help, which is #1 in the "7 Cool T" principles I'll share with you in Chapter 5. In the same chapter, I'll tell you more about how Joe got his Cool things by applying all seven of the principles, just like you can.

How does Joe Polish's <u>Cool thing</u> of buying an Arizona ghost town inspire you to do your next <u>Cool thing</u>?

Chapter 4: "The Cool thing of Transforming a $7 Yard-sale Painting into a $1,000,000 Piece of Art"

"What great thing would you attempt if you knew you could not fail?" -Robert H. Schuller

I told you in the Introduction that buying and riding a vintage scooter is cool, but it's just "small potatoes" compared to the Cool things that may be in your heart and those I'm pursuing in my business and in life. In fact, I have two that I'll tell you about in this chapter with the intent to give you further ideas and inspiration for pursuing your own.

Me at age three, paintbrush in hand

I was fortunate to be raised with a paintbrush in my hand while my dad was on his path to becoming a great full-time artist. There wasn't anything I enjoyed more as a little boy than painting with Dad at the kitchen table at night and in our basement on Saturday mornings.

Growing up, I wanted to be both a great athlete and a great artist, just like him.

This is a portrait Dad painted of me while we painted together in our basement

Now, over fifty years later, I was blessed to do the Cool thing of completing a doctoral degree at Emory University with my dissertation centered around developing a new Art Movement by merging art and theology to make social impact. I formed a nonprofit organization called Totality Ministries, to help advance this work, and at the heart of the emerging Art Movement is the $7 yard-sale painting I transformed and now offer for $1,000,000.

The "Hooding Ceremony" at Emory University during my Doctor of Ministry degree graduation

So, my next Cool things are:

1. **To sell the $1,000,000 painting**, which will help advance a new Art Movement and inspire people. I, too, believe that profit is good, but profit used for good is better. The sale of the $1 million painting will help advance much good I seek to do through my business and my nonprofit, Totality Ministries;

2. **To develop a new Art Movement called "Totalityism™"** featuring my art (the art can be seen on my website at www.PaulsonArtShow.com).

Does this sound "cool" to you? Does any of it sound "crazy or impossible?" I hope it does!

By the way, I named my nonprofit Totality Ministries because, for me, "Totality" represents people becoming totally what God created them to be, while "Ministries" is about attending to others' needs. Hence, Totality Ministries is about helping people become total, which includes helping them do Cool things.

"Art Movements"

I think of the Cool things Buck Paulson, Sy Sperling, Joe Polish, and I have each done and are seeking to do, and I'm excited about you achieving more of your own. With mine, I'm aware that people don't just go around starting new Art Movements, and I respect that they happen organically over time. Yet, my next Cool thing is to develop one now.

By the way, like the definition of "cool," the definition of "Art Movement" varies depending on who you ask. It's not always clear what makes or defines one. A definition I like is the following from Vernon Hyde Minor's book Art History's History:

> "An art movement is a style of art with a specified objective and philosophy that is adopted and followed by a group of artists during a specific period that may span from a few months to years or decades" (Minor, 2001, p. 128).

The Art Movement I'm developing has the specific objective and philosophy of merging art and theology for social impact and philanthropy. Three areas I'm working on include: 1) helping people become all God created them to be through personal and spiritual development (including helping people get their Cool things); 2) helping to lead out in abandoning attitudes and actions of prejudice in the U.S., and 3) helping to create interfaith unity (imagine the social impact these three will make). Future areas of social impact will develop over time.

The emerging Art Movement presently features my paintings and will expand over time as I invite other artists to join me.

You've likely heard of famous Art Movements such as *Impressionism* (including works by Claude Monet), *Cubism* (including works by Picasso and Braque), *Abstract Expressionism* (including works by Pollock and Basquiat), *Harlem Renaissance* (including works by Romare Bearden), *Minimalism* (including works by Ellsworth Kelly), and others.

That's a lot of "isms."

Some of these art movements were named in derision by art critics to insult the work. For example, art critic Louis Leroy derisively coined "Impressionism" when he saw Monet's "Impression: Sunrise" painting. French art critic Louis Vauxcelles scornfully named "Cubism" in 1908 in response to George Braque's work.

"If you want to do something great, stop waiting for permission."

Again, I respect the time-honored process of Art Movements emerging organically over time. However, I do not wish to wait for someone at some point in the future to identify and name the Art Movement that I'm working to develop for good now. My approach is informed by Dr. Martin Luther King, Jr. who spoke of "the fierce urgency of now." The work is too important to wait, and I feel an urgency to help see the social impact I seek to come to fruition. If you, too, want to achieve something great, don't wait; take initiative and act.

An example of what I'm doing to move forward without waiting for permission is advancing the following report from an Emmy Award-winning writer, a Master of Journalism graduate from the University of Maryland who happens to be my daughter, Jenny Provance. The cover page reads, "Introducing: The New Art Movement of the 21st

Century" – Totalityism – A developing Art Movement created by Dr. Timothy Paulson."

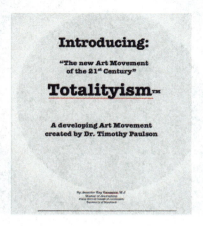

The second page refers to "The Art Movement with Social Impact."

As I've studied art history, I've never heard of anyone just deciding to start an Art Movement like I'm working to do. I'm attempting to "flip the script" by proactively working to develop "Totalityism" because of its profound importance today.

My "Totality" painting (36"x36") helps represent the Totalityism Art Movement

"How the former $7 yard-sale painting now priced at $1,000,000 is important to you"

I've met with mixed reactions when telling the story of my transformation of the $7 yard-sale painting. Some think the "drip" technique I painted it in is ugly and by extension, they think my painting is ugly. Others are dubious about my pricing the painting at a million bucks; to them, it seems silly or ridiculous. But to many others, the painting is beautiful and electrifying, and they are excited about its vibrancy, story, purpose, price, and role in the emerging Art Movement.

Selling the painting will result in the following:

1. Again, the sale will help fund and advance the emergence of the Totalityism Art Movement. The news and publicity of the sale will

help bring attention to the movement and its objectives to make major social impact.

2. The sale of the painting will serve as a powerful real-life example to those who want to achieve the "impossible" in business and in their personal life. Defining and seeing an Art Movement emerging could be tricky to "wrap your arms around." But the sale of a million-dollar painting is tangible. Saying, "The painting sold for $1 million" will provide clear evidence that <u>Cool things</u> come to fruition. When the painting sells, I hope it goes to your heart and <u>you</u> say to yourself, "If Timothy can get that <u>Cool thing</u>, surely I can get my <u>Cool thing</u> too," and believe it. It will be a vivid example that the seemingly impossible can happen.

"Rise from the Dust"
– the $1,000,000 painting –

"Rise from the Dust" (36"x48")

In case you're wondering, yes, I do expect the million-dollar painting to sell. And I hope the future buyer will consider loaning the painting at times to art museums around the U.S. and beyond so more people can view it and be inspired by its story. It will be associated with the emerging Art Movement, and I expect the sale of the painting to serve as a catalyst for significant social impact.

The $1 million painting, "Rise from the Dust," on display

"Let's scare some people"

Dr. R. Kendall Soulen was my brilliant doctoral advisor at Emory University. After I gave my final speech to conclude my doctoral program (pictured below), Professor Soulen stated to me and the audience that after having advised doctoral students for many years, my project (to develop an Art Movement to help abandon attitudes and actions of prejudice in the U.S., sell the $1 million painting, etc.) was <u>by far the most ambitious he'd ever seen and that my project scared him.</u>

Giving my final speech in my DMin program
(photo courtesy of Dr. Jason Ratliff)

Dr. Soulen's comments helped illuminate for me #4 of the "7 Cool T" principles: "Scare some people," which I'll fully discuss in Chapter 5. I thanked Dr. Soulen for his comments, and I am even more determined to bring my work to full fruition.

Dr. R. Kendall Soulen and me

> **"When's the best time to plant a tree? 25 years ago. When's the next best time to plant a tree? Today."**
>
> -Chinese Proverb

I earned my doctorate at the age of 62. I started late, but I finished what some people thought was crazy and even impossible for me to accomplish. The point is there doesn't have to be an expiration date to achieve your next <u>Cool thing</u> in your business and in your personal life. Go ahead and start – it's not too early or too late to go after your next <u>Cool thing</u> now, and it doesn't matter what other people think.

In the next chapter, I'll tell you how Buck, Sy, Joe, and I are getting <u>Cool things</u> by applying all of the "<u>7 Cool T</u>" principles – and how you can, too.

In what ways can my <u>Cool things</u> inspire your next <u>Cool thing</u>?

Chapter 5: "Introducing the '7 Cool T' Principles & a Case Study"

> "To live through an impossible situation,
> you don't need to have the reflexes of
> a Grand Prix driver, the muscles of
> a Hercules, the mind of an Einstein.
> You simply need to know what to do."
>
> - Anthony Greenbank, The Book of Survival

For Buck Paulson, Sy Sperling, Joe Polish, me, and you to do the "impossible" in business and life, we need to know what to do. In this final chapter, I fully unveil the "7 Cool T" principles so you can understand how to get your next Cool thing more quickly. To help you gain more clarity on how to apply them in your life, I also include an instructive and entertaining Case Study illustrating the application of the principles in a Mexican restaurant.

The "7 Cool T" principles provide a helpful structure for business leaders, entrepreneurs, and others who want to get their next Cool thing fast. Before I go deeper into each of the principles, you should know that I didn't just pull them out of thin air, nor did I look for people and stories to fit the principles after I named them. Only after spending a lifetime with Buck Paulson and decades in the business world with Sy Sperling, Joe Polish, and others did I see commonalities and identify these principles for achieving Cool things. You don't necessarily need to implement all seven principles to accomplish the "crazy and impossible" in your business or personal life (sometimes it takes implementing just one or two), but you'll find all seven can work synergistically in helping you do so.

Of course, these seven principles are not the only traits common among high achievers. Other common traits, habits, and principles exist for entrepreneurs, business leaders, and others (such as those identified in the books <u>7 Habits of Highly Effective People</u> and <u>Think & Grow Rich</u>). However, as I look at the lives of Elon Musk, Gandhi, Mother Teresa, Harriet Tubman, MLK, Joseph Smith, Jr., and others who have achieved some of the "Coolest things" I know of, I see the "<u>7 Cool T</u>" principles apparent in their successes, too.

The "7 Cool T" Principles:

1. Go to the Master
2. Do the Unexpected
3. Reinvent Something
4. Scare Some People
5. Be Different
6. Don't Wait for Permission
7. Be Decisive

In various ways, I've already illuminated the seven principles in the stories I've shared about Buck, Sy, Joe, and myself. I here set them apart and give additional insights into each.

1. "The Go to the Master Principle™"

Whatever "crazy or impossible" thing you want to accomplish, you can find a master who can help. Regardless of what it is, there's someone who can give you direction, confidence, secrets, and encouragement to accomplish it. The master could be a coach, teacher, trainer, speaker, consultant, pastor or bishop, author, advisor, mentor, parent, or some other expert. "Going to the master" with a burning desire may be the single most effective shortcut to doing your Cool thing fast, as is shown in the following examples.

Buck Paulson went to a master coach, Danny Litwhiler, to speed his ascent into professional baseball. Years later, Buck providentially met Kitty West, who said, "If you want to learn to paint, go to the master. His name is Claude Buck." Her suggestion resonated with Dad, and he went straight to the master, who confidently said, "Let's see if we can make a great artist out of you in a year," which came to fruition with Claude's help. And now, Buck Paulson is the master artist countless people have gone to over the years for painting instruction.

When **Sy Sperling** went to Berton Miller, a master of the craft of producing TV commercials, it was Bert who came up with the famous tag-line that made Hair Club for Men a household name: "I'm not only the Hair Club president, but I'm also a client." Had Sy not gone to the master, his business would have done well, but it would not have become the $120 million a year business it did without the iconic tag-line along with Sy's involvement in the commercials.

Joe Polish was a young, dead-broke Carpet Cleaner living off credit cards before discovering two of the masters in the field of marketing, namely Gary Halbert and Dan Kennedy. Joe sought them out, invested heavily in time and money to get their help, and <u>quickly</u> became highly successful in business by learning and applying marketing insights from the masters. Joe has continued seeking masters in all aspects of business, health, addiction recovery, and other areas important to him and the entrepreneurs he serves. He also involved masters of real estate investing and development to help him buy Cleator. To me, one of the biggest and most apparent reasons for Joe's success is that he's gone to the masters in areas he's wanted help. He has spent millions of dollars doing so, which has been one of his best investments. Joe is now the master that high-level entrepreneurs flock to from around the world by joining his <u>Genius Network</u> and <u>100K Group</u>.

I grew up with a paintbrush in my hand, learning to paint from my dad, a master artist in his own right. I later looked to the work of a master from the past when considering how to convert a $7 yard-sale painting into a dramatic and scintillating piece of art. It was Jackson Pollock who I looked to for inspiration as I studied his work. Pollock's "drip" technique paintings have sold for some of the highest prices ever recorded, including his "Number 5 1948" painting that sold for an incredible $140 million in a Christie's auction in 2006. The piece of art I created with the "drip" technique is priced at a comparable bargain – "just" $1 million!

Some of the most significant <u>Cool things</u> in life are spiritual, and going to the master can be spiritual, too. As mentioned, the new Art Movement I'm working to develop merges art and theology, and I titled the $1 million painting <u>Rise from the Dust</u> for three reasons. First, it literally rose from the dust of a yard sale as a $7 painting;

second, it represents people rising up to become all God created them to be; and third, the painting and its title is a "type" of Christ rising from the tomb on the third day. Going to the Master, Jesus Christ, helps us rise up to meet life's challenges, grow and become better, and hastens every good thing in life. If you genuinely want to do the impossible in life, go to the Master ("I can do all things through Christ who strengthens me" [Philippians 4:13]). By going to Him, my life is full and wonderful because my faith in Him is strong, my marriage is amazing, my family is united and full of love, and my purpose on earth is clear. I love the Savior, and his birth, perfect life, atonement, death on the cross, and resurrection are, in the words of this book, the coolest things ever! I seek to accomplish <u>Cool things</u> to ultimately bring glory to Him.

Who is the master you can go to for help to achieve your Cool thing?

2. "The Reinvent Something Principle™"

My wife and I collect antiques and enjoy reinventing old items for new uses. Kay uses antiques to creatively decorate our home for every season of the year. And as I've shown, I use my vintage scooter in a reinvented way – to help promote my art. As it turns out, reinventing something can be helpful in your quest to accomplish your Cool thing, as you'll see in the following examples.

My "Statue of Liberty" painting with my vintage scooter, reinvented to "frame" my paintings.

Buck Paulson helped in the reinvention of the delivery of painting instruction in the world. For decades, Dad taught students in person in his art studio, in workshops around North America, and even in Dubai. Then in 1988, he began teaching on television with his own PBS television show, helping to prepare the way for him and other artists to reach and teach millions more people.

It's not hyperbole when I tell you that **Sy Sperling** reinvented the men's hair replacement industry. When the rest of the industry sold "hair replacement," Sy offered "The Strand-by-Strand System®." Instead of naming his company something like "Sy's Hair Replacement," he called it <u>Hair Club for Men</u>. Before Sy came along, men's hair replacement was kind of a back-room type of industry. Sy made it more welcomed and acceptable for men to feel good about improving their appearance. Many people in the industry have told me that having Hair Club as a competitor was the best thing that ever happened to their business because Sy made men doing something about their appearance positive and even exciting, which had a ripple effect on the rest of the industry.

Joe Polish is reinventing the town of Cleator, taking it from a sleepy little ghost town and turning it into an interesting and dynamic destination. As mentioned, he and his partners have remodeled the old schoolhouse and turned it into a state-of-the-art event center, and put Cleator into "Virtual Reality." They've also launched Cleator-themed products like "Cleator Honey," and plans are for Cleator to even appear in a popular comic book series.

As you might expect, a favorite example of the "Reinvent something" principle is **my taking the $7 yard-sale painting** and transforming it from a dull landscape into a dynamic and exciting abstract painting now priced at $1,000,000. The reinvention of the painting has been part of speeches I've given, coaching I've done, articles I've written, and the story has now appeared in multiple books.

This is a picture from inside the Cleator Schoolhouse before renovations. Joe and his partners gave me the old desk in the photo, which now sits in my art studio

Here, the Cleator school desk is in my art studio, holding the $1,000,000 painting

I appreciate this "Reinvent Something Principle" that has played out so significantly in my life.

What can you do to "reinvent" something on the path to achieving your <u>Cool thing</u>?

3. "The Do the Unexpected Principle™"

Buying my vintage scooter unexpectedly set me on an upward trajectory of creativity that helped me to achieve the Cool thing of writing this book. Doing the unexpected is something that, as you'll see in the following examples, can make a significant impact on your life, too.

Buck Paulson unexpectedly pivoted from being a professional athlete to later becoming a great artist. The unexpected statement by Claude Buck, "Let's see if we can make a great artist out of you in a year," set Dad on the path and was the catalyst for achieving his next Cool thing. It was unexpected to my mom, who had three kids who were two years old and younger at the time, when Dad told her he wanted to be an artist. I'm sure she was happy with Dad's secure job as a Supervisor in the Santa Barbara Recreation Department at the time. Dad did the unexpected, Mom completely supported the idea, and his becoming a great full-time artist is one of the coolest things I've ever witnessed.

Sy Sperling went on TV commercials showing his "before" picture and saying his famous tagline, "I'm not only the Hair Club president, but I'm also a client." The tagline with the unveiling of his "before" photo was so unexpected that millions of people paid attention and responded to the commercials over the years. Sy hadn't expected to appear in his commercials, but by doing so, he became a household name and his tagline became iconic.

Joe Polish did the unexpected by buying a 40-acre ghost town – I and many others were blown away when he bought Cleator. Today, owning the town is one of Joe's Cool things, and its unexpectedness has attracted much attention and stimulated many people's imaginations and excitement for Joe's businesses and events, including Genius Network.

I did the unexpected by pricing the former $7 yard-sale painting at $1,000,000. I'm not aware of any precedent for this, and no one suggested I do it. I just did it, and I hope we'll see the painting sell because it'll be a catalyst for so much good in the world. And, as I've already mentioned multiple times, I'm doing the unexpected by working to develop a new Art Movement as well.

Finally, it was unexpected to my friends, colleagues, and family when I went to Liberty University's School of Divinity to earn two Masters degrees and to Emory University's School of Theology to earn a Doctor of Ministry degree. Some people wondered if I was doing it to enter the paid ministry (that was not the reason). Some pastor friends from various faith groups in my cohort at Emory University were surprised that I, a member of The Church of Jesus Christ of Latter-day Saints, a church without a paid ministry, would earn the graduate degrees that professional clergy seek. Frankly, it was totally unexpected to me, too, when I felt God direct me to earn these degrees. It didn't make a lot of sense at the time, but I'm forever grateful I was directed to do so. The education and degrees I've gained have enhanced my life, including helping lead me to write this book.

Doing the unexpected draws attention to what you're doing and stimulates action. Simply put, it's a solid approach that can help you achieve your next Cool thing.

What's something "unexpected" you can do to help you on the path to achieving your <u>Cool thing</u>?

4. "The Scare Some People Principle™"

The fourth of the "<u>7 Cool T</u>" principles was brought to light by Dr. Soulen, my doctoral advisor who, as I mentioned in Chapter 4, stated after my final presentation that my project was by far the most ambitious he'd ever seen in all his years working with doctoral students, and it scared him. This "Scare some people principle" is about having high ambition and taking risks to draw attention and to light a fire for achieving your <u>Cool thing</u>. This principle also includes <u>scaring yourself</u> because if you are not scared, you may not be going after something "crazy or impossible" after all. Pursuing your <u>Cool thing</u> can be scary to you because you'll be doing things you likely haven't done before. Becoming a professional baseball player and a full-time professional artist, building a business empire, buying a ghost town, pricing and attempting to sell a $1 million painting, developing a new Art Movement, along with <u>you</u> doing the <u>Cool thing</u> in your heart – it all can be scary. It's important to embrace being scared, learn to "dance with it," and allow it to be a catalyst for action, growth, and accomplishment.

Buck Paulson's ambition to become a full-time artist surely scared people who wondered why a total sports jock would risk his livelihood and leave his secure job at the Recreation Department to become a full-time artist. Doing something scary paid off as he has been a full-time artist for the past 54 years, and today, at the age of 90, he continues to teach and produce beautiful work.

Sy Sperling scared some people around him when he did things so differently than the rest of the industry, and took the risk of putting vast amounts of money and his reputation on the line as he went forward with the major expansion of <u>Hair Club for Men</u>. Sy did a lot of scary things, but his ambition and risk paid off as he built an incredible $120 million-a-year company.

Joe Polish's high ambition and tolerance for risk have, at times, been scary but also a force for him doing remarkable things in his career. For example, buying a ghost town – to some, that's risky and scary. But Joe has done things with the town already and will continue to boggle people's minds with what he does in the future to help improve lives and enhance the entrepreneurial journey through Cleator.

Me pricing a painting at $1 million is ambitious – so much that it scares people who think I'm crazy. However, when people visit my art gallery, the "Rise from the Dust" painting gets the most attention and creates the most excitement by far. When I speak at seminars, make posts in social media, and meet and talk with people in a variety of settings, the $1 million painting is what they want to talk about.

What can you do that's so ambitious and even risky that it scares you and others on the way to getting your <u>Cool thing</u>?

5. "The Be Different Principle"

Throughout this book, I've repeated, "Being different is better than being better" several times. Buck Paulson, Sy Sperling, Joe Polish, and I have all found ways to differentiate ourselves and our businesses. I've already discussed the value of being different in some detail in the first four chapters. I'll briefly add a bit more color to the principle in the following examples:

Buck Paulson was different by showing a burning desire and determination when he resigned from his job and became a full-time artist when he had a wife and very young kids to provide for. I wrote about how Dad is different as an artist in Chapter 1. I've always been impressed that he had the boldness to ask his master artist instructor, Claude Buck, if he could use his name as part of his artist name, as in Buck Paulson, after just completing his very first painting with him. The distinct and bold name Buck Paulson has become well known and has always helped set him apart as different.

Sy Sperling's Hair Club for Men was different from any other hair company, as I detailed in Chapter 2. He appeared in his television commercials with a now iconic tagline; the company name was different; the way the company spoke of the hair and its process was different; and the offices and employees were different.

In Chapter 3, I told you ways **Joe Polish** has differentiated himself. Additionally, as I mentioned earlier, the purchase of Cleator came with a Yacht Club right in the middle of the desert, with no body of water within 50 miles! If you ever visit Cleator, you'll see old boats, jet skis, and surfboards in an area behind the General Store known as the "Cleator Bar & Yacht Club." Surprisingly, thousands of people have "joined the Yacht Club" by giving their name and contact info as they pass through because it's fun and different.

The Cleator General Store is pictured on top, and part of the Yacht Club is also pictured and includes an old boat and surfboard tables sitting in the desert

My art is different, too. My dad's teacher, Claude Buck, was part of an American Artist's society in the 1930s and 1940s called "Sanity in Art," with its members opposed to all forms of modern art, including Abstract Expressionism, Surrealism, and Cubism. The society members didn't like what they viewed as the "insane" styles of Pollock, Picasso, and other artists of their ilk. Dad was taught by Claude Buck to paint in the beautiful "Old Master" style which involves representational painting, and Dad has skillfully advanced the style for many years. Conversely, I absolutely love modern art, and I choose to paint in a style that explodes with color, often with abstract and impressionistic characteristics. My work tends to be more textured, expressive, colorful, and soulful than traditional art. Take my *Beatles Sculpture* painting, for example; it's different because I painted "John, Paul, Ringo, and George" on a tree stump that I rescued from a campfire in the mountains of Utah. It's now a unique three-dimensional piece of art.

My "Beatles Sculpture" sitting on
the back of my vintage scooter

My $1 million painting also stands out as different because it started out as a dusty, dull, and forgotten $7 yard-sale painting that I transformed into something exciting that people talk about. The painting is different because of its backstory, purpose, and meaning – and because of its price.

Not only is my art different, but I strive to be different, too. I'm not the best entrepreneur, artist, speaker, or author, nor the most gifted Doctor of Ministry – but I'm different because I combine art, speaking, writing, and theology in the work I do. Again, "it's better to be different than it is to be better."

How can you be DIFFERENT on the path to achieving your Cool thing?

6. "The Don't Wait for Permission Principle™"

Are you waiting for permission to accomplish something "crazy or impossible?" You can break through roadblocks with the "Don't Wait for Permission Principle" that can lead you to "unmined gold," personally and financially, as you'll see in the following examples.

Buck Paulson didn't wait for someone to give him permission to aggressively pursue becoming a professional baseball player or to begin painting when it just didn't seem to make sense. Despite some saying he wasn't cut out for pro baseball or art; he went after and got both <u>Cool things</u>.

Sy Sperling didn't wait for permission to reinvent the hair replacement industry and create a business empire; he just did it. Some told Sy he shouldn't "rock the boat" and should "go with the flow" in the industry, while some in the industry became resentful and jealous of him. But Sy wasn't concerned – he gave himself permission, and as a result, he accomplished his <u>Cool thing</u> of creating a business empire.

Joe Polish didn't wait for permission to buy Cleator – he just did it. And Joe isn't waiting for permission to mine for gold there, either. Gold mines near Cleator were said to have been depleted by the end of the 19th century, but how could they have known over 100 years ago that all the gold was discovered? Joe and his partners <u>own mining rights</u> in Cleator and have plans to mine for gold again. In so doing, they're doing the unexpected. They're not waiting for permission to do the remarkable – they're just moving forward to do another <u>Cool thing</u>.

I, too, give myself permission. I gave myself permission to price a painting at $1 million. I gave myself permission to start my business in 1995. I gave myself permission to work to develop a new Art Movement. I gave myself permission to write books. I gave myself permission to name and introduce to you the "7 Cool T" principles to provide structure and instruction for getting your own Cool thing. If I had waited for someone else to give me permission to do any of these things, little would have happened.

Of course, there are exceptions. For example, you can't just walk in and perform surgery in a hospital without permission, walk on the field and play center field for the LA Dodgers without permission, nor can you walk in and fly a commercial airplane without permission.

The "Don't Wait for Permission Principle" is about having the attitude and determination that you're not going to sit back and wait for something to happen – you're taking action to make things happen within moral and ethical parameters.

I repeat my question: Are you waiting for permission to accomplish something "crazy or impossible?" I invite you to move forward to get your Cool thing by applying the "Don't Wait for Permission Principle."

Where and how can you give yourself permission to do your <u>Cool thing</u>?

7. "The Be Decisive Principle"

Napoleon Hill wrote the classic book Think & Grow Rich in 1937. Hill, who closely studied the billionaire Andrew Carnegie and hundreds of the world's most successful people in the early 20th century, included a chapter titled "DECISION." He taught that a common characteristic of the most successful people in the world is that they are decisive.

Being decisive is clearly part of getting your Cool thing as I've shown in each of the first four chapters of this book. From baseball, art, a business empire, an Arizona ghost town, developing a new Art Movement, selling a $1 million painting and so forth, Buck Paulson, Sy Sperling, Joe Polish, and I are decisive.

When I felt the seemingly crazy spiritual impression to go back to school at an advanced age to get a Master of Divinity degree from Liberty University, I wondered how my wife would feel about it. When I spoke with her, her response was priceless: **"I definitely think you should do that. How quickly can you start?"** Kay, too, was decisive, which helped me to confidently move forward.

I mentioned that I was able to buy the vintage scooter only after someone else was indecisive and missed out. An individual interested in buying the town of Cleator, AZ, missed out by not being decisive and immediately regretted it. I wonder what "Cool thing" you may be missing out on right now by not being more decisive. When we procrastinate and "think about it" over and over, we miss out. I invite you to be more decisive so you don't miss out on getting your Cool thing.

How can you be more DECISIVE on the path to achieving your Cool thing?

"A '7 Cool T' Principles Case Study":
A Mexican Restaurant Owner named Bent

On the cover of this book it says, "How a $1 Million Painting, a Vintage Scooter, an Arizona Ghost Town, and Guacamole Can Help You Do Your Impossible 'Cool Thing' Fast." I'm about to share a Case Study that will deliver on the "Guacamole" part of that statement.

I've been in the business world for over four decades and could have chosen from scores of different examples of "crazy and impossible" things I've seen being achieved to share with you. In addition to what I've already written about in Chapters 1-4, I've chosen a Case Study you'll be able to relate to, and that will be highly instructive because it's about a smart, talented, and determined entrepreneur who faced and overcame major challenges.

Bent Hansen is a restaurant owner whose actions to get his Cool thing during the problematic time of COVID are illustrative of the seven principles. Bent has done other Cool things before and after COVID, and I could have written about one or more of those. But what he did during the pandemic is so instructive that I've chosen to share his story as a valuable Case Study.

Bent Hansen at his Los Gringos Locos restaurant during COVID (photo courtesy of Bent Hansen)

Bent Hansen was born and raised in Boise, Idaho, where his family entered the restaurant business with "Poco a Poco Restaurant" in 1972. With entrepreneurism in his blood, Bent later moved to Southern California, where he has owned Los Gringos Locos, a Mexican Restaurant in La Cañada, since 1996. I've been to the restaurant multiple times, and it boasts some of the best Mexican food I've had. The Grilled Flautas served "Bent style" (it comes with a unique "money back guarantee") and the "World Famous Tableside Guacamole" are my favorite menu items there.

Me at <u>Los Gringos Locos</u>, enjoying
the Grilled Flautas served "Bent Style"
(photo by Ted Shredd)

During COVID, restrictions on restaurants in California were among the strictest in the country. The state came down hard, making it difficult for many restaurants to even stay open. The restrictions initially included not being able to offer indoor dining, which, for Bent, meant either becoming a 100% takeout and delivery restaurant or closing the restaurant. Bent's restaurant is located in a shopping center and doesn't have a drive-through. However, while other restaurants in the area closed (unfortunately, some permanently), Bent stayed the course.

Bent's "crazy and impossible" ambition – his <u>Cool thing</u> – was clear: "<u>Los Gringos Locos</u> will not only survive but will thrive during the COVID shutdown." His ambition scared some people who thought he was taking too many risks and was overly optimistic, but he was determined.

A key for Bent was to not focus on restrictions with the question "What **can't** we do?" but instead focus on opportunities by asking, "What **can** we do?"

Bent instinctively implemented each of the "7 Cool T" Principles:

- He went to the master
- He did the unexpected
- He reinvented something
- He scared some people
- His business was different
- He didn't wait for permission
- He was decisive

Here's how Bent implemented each of the "7 Cool T" principles:

#1: Go to the master: Bent is innovative, talented, open-minded, and creative, and understands the value of going to the master. I met Bent in 2006 when he went to the master, Rory Fatt, a brilliant coach, marketer and business innovator, by joining Rory's Platinum Elite mastermind group that I help lead. We've been masterminding with Bent for almost two decades now, and I've witnessed first-hand that any degree of pride, or an "I know it all" attitude, is entirely foreign to Bent. He is teachable and open to and appreciates input from others. In fact, when Bent was moving his restaurant from its original location to its current larger location in 2012, he came to the group, showed us the written drawings and plans for the build-out of the new restaurant, and asked for input for making the plans better for a more efficient and guest-friendly dining experience. Rory and the group were so helpful in this that Bent refers to Los Gringos Locos as "the restaurant Platinum Elite helped build."

Bent's "going to the master" intensified during COVID. Rory and Platinum Elite were of invaluable help to Bent and the other members during the shutdown, and some of the members credit the group for helping save their business during that time. Insights and encouragement were freely shared on frequent group mastermind calls via Zoom to advise and encourage each other during dark and harrowing times. In mastermind sessions, Bent formulated plans, got feedback on his ideas, shared valuable insights with others, and determined to continue to move forward. It takes humility to recognize you can't do it alone and to "go to the master" for help. Bent did, and you can, too.

#2: Do the unexpected: Bent did the unexpected by even staying open for business during COVID. When the restrictions on restaurants operating were first announced, many people assumed Los Gringos Locos would just shut down. But Bent kept the business open and found ways to keep his staff employed when letting them go seemed to make more sense. One of the unexpected things Bent did was something called "In the Alley," a special he occasionally offered to his guests. They felt like "insiders" when Bent emailed and texted them that they could, almost in "prohibition" style, go to the alley behind the restaurant and buy a prepared meal that was unexpectedly not Mexican food – it was a complete Prime Rib dinner! Bent hired a small band to play music off to the side while car after car drove up, paid a good price, enjoyed the live music, picked up their bagged Prime Rib dinner, and drove off. Hence, while delicious Mexican food was offered inside the restaurant, something completely different and unexpected was quietly available in the alley, which was both good for business and a big hit with Bent's guests.

You can see the alley as it usually looks in the photo on the top left, the set-up for the "In the Alley" offer in the photo on the top right, and the band playing in the corner in the above photo

Bent did something else unexpected when he recognized people missed connecting with others and were looking for something to do during COVID – he created virtual beverage tastings. The way it worked was that people would come to the restaurant to buy a customized and branded "full tasting kit" handmade by Bent's staff. Then, at home, they watched an expert hired by Bent show them via Zoom how to prepare and enjoy the beverages in different ways, including with chocolate, spiced salt, lemon, orange, etc. The participants made new friends, enjoyed the entertainment, loved a sense of community, and had fun as they interacted virtually with the experts and with each other.

#3: Reinvent something: Los Gringos Locos restaurant's most popular and profitable menu item is its "World Famous Tableside Guacamole," made in a fun and entertaining way by a "Guacamole Master" on a guacamole cart rolled right up to the guest tables. (By the way, guacamole made tableside on a cart was invented by Bent's Los Gringos Locos restaurant in June 1996, as reported in the culinary magazine "Saveur" [in its November '22 edition].) During COVID, the environment for restaurants in the LA area was chaotic, with new rules and regulations coming down and changing from week to week. After some time, indoor dining was allowed, but unfortunately, buffets and tableside items were outlawed. Thus, Bent's #1 most popular and profitable menu item couldn't be offered under the restrictions. But this did not stop Bent. He reinvented it so that the Guacamole Master made "tableside guacamole" – from a separate location in the restaurant.

Here's how it worked. The waitstaff rolled out to the tables a guacamole cart with a TV monitor, microphone, and speaker on it. Guests could see and interact with the Guacamole Master on-screen as their guacamole was made in a studio out of sight. It was a genius reinvention, and "Tableside Guacamole" remained the top menu item, even during the COVID shutdown.

Bent brilliantly reinvented "Tableside Guacamole" to have it made in a studio in another part of the restaurant (photo courtesy of Bent Hansen)

This reinvention was instrumental in <u>Los Gringos Locos</u> prospering during the COVID shutdown. <u>Doing what Bent did, not literally with guacamole, but figuratively by reinventing something</u>, can be transformational in the quest for your <u>Cool thing</u>, too.

#4: Scare some people: Some family, friends, and guests were scared that Bent was a little "loco" by risking so much by staying open during COVID. They were scared that Bent was making a big mistake by retaining employees. Bent has a big heart and didn't want to put any employee in a difficult financial position by letting them go, so he kept all who wanted to stay. There were also times when some close to him were scared that he was pushing some of the government restrictions. Bent took risks, scared some people, and embraced any fear he personally felt, which, it turns out, is a solid principle in getting <u>Cool things</u>.

#5: Be different: Indoor dining was initially not allowed in the LA area, so Bent recognized an opportunity to be different and ordered large outdoor open-air tents that were put up in the shopping center parking lot outside his restaurant. Under the tents, he could deliver food to guests who could come and sit and be served outside. Bent also created a dining area in a walkway between two buildings in the shopping center about 75 yards from the restaurant. Tables in the tents and in the walkway were set up a distance apart with glass partitions in between as the state required.

Los Gringos Locos initially moved to outdoor dining under tents in the parking lot (photos courtesy of Bent Hansen)

Bent converted the open breezeway that I'm pictured in on the top photo into a "Fresco" during COVID

While other restaurants either closed or struggled, Bent found ways to be different, and under the circumstances, his restaurant thrived. Remember, "It's good to be better, but it's better to be different." Bent was both better and different.

#6: Don't wait for permission: Because I spoke regularly with Bent in group mastermind Zoom sessions during the COVID shutdown, I got "blow-by-blow" accounts of what he was up to. While many businesses were paralyzed by confusion and uncertainty about what they could and couldn't do, often waiting for permission to do something, Bent had the attitude that it was "the Wild West" and he just took action.

Information coming down was often contradictory, with rules seemingly being made up by regulatory agencies on the fly. Bent could have chosen to sit around, waiting for someone to give him more clarity on everything, but he didn't. He pushed the limits within the constantly changing boundaries as he understood them. Like Bent, "If you want to do something great, stop waiting for permission."

#7: Be decisive: I'm a witness to seeing Bent decide, right from the beginning, that he would relentlessly work to have a restaurant that would thrive during the pandemic. He was decisive about going to the master Rory Fatt and his <u>Platinum Elite</u> mastermind group, doing the unexpected, reinventing things, being an ambitious risk taker who scared some people, being different, and not waiting for permission.

The rest of the story is that Bent did indeed get his <u>Cool thing</u>. In 2021, "Trip Advisor" named <u>Los Gringos Locos</u> the **#14 "Best of the Best" restaurant nationally** and **#1 out of 38 restaurants locally**. I'm not the only one impressed with Bent – in 2022, he was awarded the La Cañada **"Business Owner of the Year"** because he navigated the business so successfully through COVID.

Though Bent has a casual and laid-back demeanor, he shows the same determination Buck Paulson had in becoming a pro baseball player and a great artist; he has a vision and is an aggressive marketer like Sy Sperling in building his business empire; he's not afraid to do unexpected things like Joe Polish does in his business and in buying a ghost town; he doesn't wait for permission in the same way I haven't in pricing my $1 million painting and working to develop a new Art Movement.

I chose to share this Case Study because it's instructive, and it's good for you to know the principles are potent even during unusual times. Bent's not a famous celebrity, a great artist, a legendary business figure (yet), or the buyer of a ghost town, but he regularly does extraordinary things in his business. I've shown how Bent implemented the "7 Cool T" principles before I even identified them. I hope his story inspires you to relentlessly go after your next Cool thing, too.

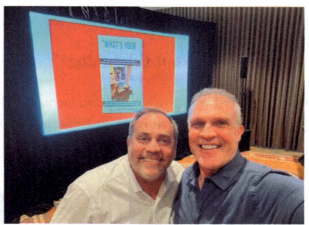

Bent Hansen and me at a seminar in Nashville where I spoke on the topic of "What's your Cool thing?"

By the way, Bent not only implements the "7 Cool T" principles, but he and his wife, Joy, also own five scooters. Now that's cool!

Conclusion

"In a year that has been so improbable,
the impossible has happened!"

-Vin Scully, LA Dodgers announcer,
after Kirk Gibson's historic home run
in game 1 of the 1988 World Series

I conclude by repeating the question I asked earlier:

"What's your Cool thing?"

I return to what I shared with you in the Introduction of this book – the incredulous yet eager comment from the brilliant John Raymonds to Peter Diamandis, founder of the XPRIZE, shown in the following art:

I hope this book has helped you move toward the "crazy and impossible" – the Cool thing you seek in your business or personal life – by illustrating how the "7 Cool T" principles are manifest in the successes of Buck Paulson, Sy Sperling, Joe Polish, Bent Hansen, and myself. Further, as you consider some of the colossal accomplishments in history by world famous high achievers, I believe you'll find the "7 Cool T" principles manifest in their successes, too.

Lastly, this may be one of the shortest "self-help" type books you've ever read, and some will dismiss it because of its length and simplicity. However, I hope you have enjoyed the quick read and appreciate the stories and examples of the $1 million painting, my vintage scooter, the Arizona ghost town, tableside guacamole, and much more to help illustrate how the "7 Cool T" principles can help you get your "impossible" Cool thing fast.

What's your next Cool thing for your business?

What's your next Cool thing for your personal life?

There may not be a better time than now to go after them.

"Let's go!"

"Who is Timothy Paulson?"

My favorite <u>Cool thing</u> is being married to my beautiful wife, Kay, since 1983. Another is being the father of our five fabulous kids (Jenny, TJ, Jake, Cara Lyn, and Courtney), father-in-law to four remarkable individuals (Adam, Meredith, Kate, and Brian), and "Pop" to our 12 wonderful and beautiful grandkids.

I've been self-employed since 1995, and have been fortunate to be a featured speaker in business seminars worldwide, including in Cairo, Sydney, London, Dublin, Vancouver, Toronto, Mexico, the Bahamas, and throughout the USA. I'm an artist, author, coach, speaker, and devout Christian. I have a bachelor's degree in Business Management and two biblically-based master's degrees, and I earned a Doctor of Ministry degree from Emory University in Atlanta.

Kay and me at Emory University during graduation

Thank you for reading. Please send me a note to let me know about the <u>Cool things</u> you achieve in your business and in your life. I'll be happy to hear from you.

Paulson Creativity Studio, LLC
& <u>Totality Ministries</u>
P.O. Box 41
Tremonton, UT 84337
www.PaulsonArtShow.com

Made in the USA
Columbia, SC
08 February 2025

53548605R00063